Tynemouth
in old picture postcards

by E.J. Hollerton

European Library ZALTBOMMEL/THE NETHERLANDS

GB ISBN 90 288 3496 6

© 1987 European Library – Zaltbommel/The Netherlands

Fourth edition, 1997: reprint of the original edition of 1987.

INTRODUCTION

Perched high above the North Sea, its wide main street leading to the Castle gate, Tynemouth Village probably owes its existence to the Benedictine Priory and the later fortifications. The pilgrims of the Middle Ages, seeking the shrine of Saint Oswin, would certainly have attracted people to settle near the monastery. The castle, built to protect the Tyne from the insurrections and Scottish wars which bedevilled the North, would have been a source of comfort to many. As time passed, and the country became more settled, the castle's importance grew less immediate. By the end of the eighteenth century the bulk of the population in the area lived on the cramped banksides of the industrial town of North Shields. Wind-swept, open, and largely free of the manufacturing and poor sanitation of the Tyneside towns, the village began to attract those who could travel, as a health resort. The popularisation of sea-bathing, by the Prince Regent, and the discovery of a chalybeate spring, would certainly have helped Tynemouth's growth. There was even a certain amount of feedback from the visitors. Harriet Martineau published her 'Letters from the Sick-Room' whilst staying at Tynemouth from 1839 to 1844. She contributed to the health of the village by draining the main street, and providing a well. In another instance, William Scott, a regular visitor, erected a fountain in 1861.

The villagers encouraged visitors by providing lodgings, bathing-machines, and a growing range of amusements. The Fry and Linkleter families being foremost in this for over a hundred years.

By the middle of the nineteenth century the railways were serving the village. It became possible to work in Newcastle and live at the coast. With this in mind, the local landowner, the Duke of Northumberland, laid out an estate on the edge of Tynemouth. Between 1871 and 1881 the population increased by almost one third.

The Aquarium and Winter Garden, which had been intended as a draw for tourists, was not the hoped-for success, but the early 1880s saw no fall in Tynemouth's popularity. The opening of a railway line connecting Newcastle with the coastal and colliery villages, and cheap fares, made Tynemouth attractive to the growing number of excursionists. The local Council were making efforts to provide amenities, including a policeman to enforce modesty on the beaches. About this time, Matthew Auty, a tobacconist and dabbler in photography, threw up his trade to open a studio in Front Street. His views of the coast and surrounding countryside quickly became popular. Auty Limited claimed to have been the first to introduce the Continental idea of picture postcards to the north of England.

Auty's views familiarised prospective visitors with the charms of the area. The Priory, of course, was a popular subject, pictured from many angles. The Long Sands still attract thousands of visitors, despite the loss of the bathing-machines and sales booths he often recorded. The North Pier was already a popular promenade, with its views of the castle, the many ships trading in the Tyne, and even glimpses of the fishing fleet.

Along the coast and river, today's ships pass without concern the rocks and shoals which once were a source of exciting pictures. Lifeboats could be counted upon to stir the blood. The Tyne had seen the invention of the self-righting boat, and the Royal National Lifeboat Institution's first motorised craft was stationed at Tynemouth. It was also the birthplace of the Volunteer Life Brigades, and still has one of the few remaining.

Many of the quaint old cottages have been cleared away. East Street no longer clings to the cliffs over King Edward's Bay, and Percy Square was replaced by the monumental bulk of the Sir James Knott Flats.

One church is a shopping arcade and the cinema has been demolished. Tynemouth, however, continues to attract visitors to its sands and historic buildings. The village has many eating and drinking places, made accessible over a wide area by the Tyneside Metro, but still retains a few quiet corners and a sense of elegant charm.

The pictures are from the stock of the Local Studies Centre in the Old Central Library, North Shields, and the text was compiled from books, periodicals and documents in its possession. The Centre exists to preserve the records of the area currently within the Borough of North Tyneside, and to make them available to the public.

Thanks are due to all those members of the public who allowed the Local Studies Centre to copy items from their collections. Pictures from the Auty collection, numbered 16, 22, 27, 35, 45, 46, 56, 61, 63, 64, 65, 75, 81, 82, 83, 90, 91, 93, 95, 99, 109, 116, 119, 125, 127, 128, 129, 133, 134, 136, 137, 138 and 140, are included courtesy of Newcastle City Libraries. Special thanks are due to Mrs. Shirley Ellis, for her help in buying original postcards.

1. The Long Sands beach has always been one of Tynemouth's main tourist attractions. Donkeys and ponies were provided for the trippers to ride; this small herd seems to be wandering free on the rough grass banks above the beach. In the background is the neighbouring fishing village of Cullercoats, marked by the steeple of Saint George's Church. The building was erected between 1880 and 1884 at the expense of the Duke of Northumberland, in memory of his father. The large house in the centre of the picture was known as Beaconsfield.

2. A local coal-owner and philanthropist, John Henry Burn, began the building of Beaconsfield House in about 1882. He died at the turn of the century, but his widow continued in occupation for many years. One of Mister Burn's charities was the Diocesan Home for Friendless Girls, in Cullercoats, to which he contributed heavily. Given his interest in the welfare of children, he would probably have approved of the use of his house as a children's home. Doctor Barnardo's Homes bought it in 1945. Tynemouth Council purchased Beaconsfield House, and demolished it in 1957. Now only a square of earth banks marks the site.

3. In Victorian times it was the custom for tourists to bring tents and small canvas shelters to the beach. In the 1910s, however, a number of small bungalows began to appear. The local Council laid down the basic size, and the owners built their own. The differing designs, and occasional lack of maintenance in the 1920s, led the Council to worry about the effect the motley appearance would have on the attractiveness of the Long Sands. There was a plan to erect a lower promenade with purpose built chalets, but nothing came of it. In the summer of 1940, the Army took over the beach, and demolished all the old bungalows.

4. One of the earliest of the bungalows on Tynemouth Long Sands belonged to John Thomas Porter, a grocer in North Shields and an Alderman on Tynemouth Borough Council from 1916. He is seated below the verandah, holding out his golf club, and around him are his friends and family. The photograph was taken in 1914 or earlier, and Mister Porter continued to enjoy the use of the bungalow until his death in 1937. Many of the chalets were owned by people in the nearby industrial towns, and it was the custom for such parties to spend days at the beach, bringing with them their food, and anything else necessary for their pleasure.

5. South-east Northumberland is relatively flat, and before the coastal villages became dormitory towns, it was possible to see for considerable distances from Tynemouth Long Sands. From Sharpness Point the photographer looked northwards towards Whitley Village and Monkseaton. On the horizon is a steeple, which may be that of Saint Paul's Church, Whitley; it was opened in 1864. Various tourist attractions are laid out on the beach, including boats for hire, bathing-machines, and refreshment rooms.

6. In the 1860s, when most of Tynemouth was still clustered around Front Street, there was a row of wooden cottages on the Long Sands, catering to the needs of the growing tourist industry. The building to the left was Mary Ann McIntyre's; she offered lodgings. In the centre are Mrs. Frances Scott's refreshment rooms. Next is John Nicholson's cottage. A joiner and cabinet-maker, he lived there with his extensive family, and also took lodgers. At the right is an establishment which was a beerhouse run by William Coverdale, and at another time by the Roll family. Later, as a temperance café, it was occupied by a Mister Appleby. The whole row was cleared in the building of the Plaza.

7. From early in the nineteenth century people had been attracted to Tynemouth for the sea-bathing. In the interests of modesty and easy access to the water, fleets of bathing-machines began to appear. A number are parked in the foreground, at least one of which belonged to Joseph Coats, of Tynemouth, who operated in the 1880s and 1890s. At the top of the Bank is the building which came to be known as the Plaza. A gleam of glass shows that at this time it still had its original roof. The building in the background was part of the same development. When planned, it was intended to be a skating-rink, which could be flooded for use as a swimming-pool.

TYNEMOUTH PALACE

8. Late in the 1870s a ninety-year lease was obtained from the Duke of Northumberland, and the old beach cottages were cleared away. It was intended to build a new Crystal Palace as the centrepiece of a hoped-for 'Brighton of the North'. As planned, there was to be a winter garden at Promenade level, under a glass roof. Below, it would have a large aquarium, with refreshment rooms beneath, and a promenade at beach level. Tynemouth Aquarium and Winter Garden opened to the public in 1878, to short-lived success. The cost of sinking the foundations into the sand forced the sale of the building in 1880.

9. One of the few successful events of the Plaza's early life, was the North East Coast Exhibition of Naval Architecture and Marine Engineering. The organising committee had the object of gathering together examples of the state of the art in the shipping world. The response from around the country was so great that by the time the exhibition opened, on 6th September 1882, every corner of the Plaza, and its skating-rink, was filled. Exhibits ranged from boiler scale and boxes of preserved fish, through ship models and machinery, to the boat used by Grace Darling in the rescue of the 'Forfarshire'.

Tynemouth Palace Interior.

10. For much of its early life the Aquarium and Winter Garden had only limited use, and seems to have been reliant on concerts organised by the local Recreation Association. In April, 1898, the building was acquired by Mister J.F. Graham, who began work on converting the old winter garden into a theatre. As can be seen, he replaced much of the original glass roof with corrugated iron. The building was re-named the Palace Theatre. It was sold again in 1908 to a company which retained the theatre, and introduced other entertainments, including roller-skating. The growing prosperity of those years was interrupted by the Great War, during which troops were billeted in the Palace.

562

TYNEMOUTH PALACE.

11. Despite its central position on Tynemouth's Grand Parade, the Plaza was strangely unsuccessful in its early years. Shortly after it opened a horse-tram service was introduced, carrying people from the nearby town of North Shields to within a few yards of the doors. The horses were replaced by steam engines, and in 1901 a new line opened. Electric trams ran through North Shields and Tynemouth to the Plaza, and on to the villages of Cullercoats and Whitley Bay. There were even connecting services to the city of Newcastle and its suburbs. Ease of access was not the answer, however, as unenterprising owners and the building's reputation for being cold and uncomfortable seem to have kept people away.

12. In 1927 the Palace Theatre became the Plaza, under an energetic new manager, Sol Sheckman, who was later to found the Essoldo chain of cinemas. He had the Plaza extensively rebuilt, to provide a theatre and picture-house, winter garden, and café. The next year a ballroom was added, and the latest American soda-fountain. More importantly, perhaps, over two miles of heating pipes were installed, making the Plaza warm for the first time in its history. From 1933 the building was called Galaland and the Ballroom Fantastique, but Plaza is the name by which it continued to be known locally.

13. The Plaza's chequered career includes a period when it was used for billeting. During the Great War convalescent servicemen used the upper floors, but the basement was the home of the boys from the 'Wellesley' training ship. The ship was an old wooden warship moored in the Tyne at North Shields, and used as an Industrial School. Boys were trained for a life at sea and in the Forces. In March 1914, 'Wellesley' caught fire and sank at her moorings. All the officers and boys were rescued, and moved into temporary accommodations in the Tynemouth Palace. They remained there throughout the war, and afterwards, failing to buy the building for themselves, they moved to a shore station at Blyth.

14. When it was first built, it was possible to see miles of open fields from Tynemouth Plaza. The Grand Parade was still fairly new, and the railway loop-line was not opened by the North Eastern Railway Company until 1882. A small burn, known as Kenner's Dene, ran across the fields to the sea, close to the signal post in the background. In 1890 the local Council negotiated with the Duke of Northumberland the lease of a plot of seven acres of land between the railway and the Plaza. They opened a new recreation ground there in 1893, with a large pond, three bowling greens, and ornamental gardens with a bandstand. The large pavilion and tennis courts did not come into existence until 1930, after more land was leased from the Duke.

15. In the spring of 1893, as the finishing touches were being added to the pond in the new Recreation Ground, as it was known, the Council appointed a gardener to lay out the grounds. The rowing boats began as an experiment in 1908, after Dux Ferguson of Tynemouth offered to provide them for a small annual rent. The lake was the home of a number of geese and swans, and one wonders how these notoriously short-tempered birds took such an intrusion. Certainly it incensed the local model yacht club.

S 3286   TYNEMOUTH PARK FROM TOP OF PALACE.

16. Tynemouth Park was given its name in the summer of 1894. In the winter of 1892 to 1893 it was still known as the Recreation Ground. At the time large quantities of clay were being brought, to be 'puddled', in order to form the base for an ornamental lake. In November of 1893 a letter appeared in the local newspaper, offering high praise for the building of a pond. Thanks to the far-seeing and magnanimous Council, skaters would no longer have to go to an overcrowded pond at South Shields. There was a sting in the writer's tale, however, as he pointed out that the lake had been filled with salt water, which never successfully froze. Whatever happened that year, in the next winter the Council sold nearly 8,500 tickets to skaters.

17. The opening of Tynemouth Lake attracted a number of model boat enthusiasts. In the summer of 1893 an exhibition of model yachts was held in the Tynemouth Aquarium. It was promoted by the Tynemouth Recreation Association to encourage the sport. A Tynemouth Model Yacht Club was formed, and one of the first buildings planned for the Park was their boat house. The introduction of rowing boats, in 1908, so outraged them that they called on the Duke of Northumberland's agent for aid. This gentleman forced the Council to set aside longer hours when the Club might have exclusive use of the lake.

The Sands, Tynemouth

18. At the bottom of the picture is a structure surrounded by women and children. It was known far and wide as the Engine Well, and said to have given rise to the growth of Tynemouth as a health resort. The chalybeate spring became popular on Tyneside for its health-giving properties, during the 1820s. In 1863, after much delay, the local Council had an ornate well-head built over it, with a lion's head, from which the water poured. The spring was still in use in the 1920s, but there are those who say that it ceased to be popular when the water was found to come from old mine-workings. The situation cannot have been helped by the building of a stable for the beach ponies next to the well-head.

19. The distinctive strata of the cliffs identify them as Sharpness Point, even without the presence, on the horizon, of the Tynemouth Priory ruins, and the lighthouse at the end of the Tyne North Pier. The trippers are strolling the beach in the 'liberated' twentieth century. When the Tynemouth Corporation leased the Long Sands from the Duke of Northumberland in 1862, they divided the beach up with marker posts, in the interests of public decency. This southern section was allocated to female bathers only. There was a stretch of beach 100 yards wide, between them and the portion of sand to be used by males, to be kept free of all bathers.

20. Towards the turn of the century mass-produced, reliable bicycles introduced many thousands to a new form of recreation. The 'scorching' cyclist became a terror to other road users. The habit of furious riding was loudly deplored by a growing number of cycle clubs, which favoured massed runs in the countryside, as well as individual pleasure in the sport. Cycle clubs became an important part of the social life of most towns. The Borough of Tynemouth supported a number of clubs, including one for tricycles. From time to time they held parades, like the one seen on the Grand Parade at Tynemouth, during which charitable collections were taken.

21. A perennial question asked by visitors to Tynemouth relates to the large iron structure on the Long Sands. It is, in fact, the boiler of the Swedish vessel, 'Sjovik', which came ashore in bad weather during the Great War, and stuck fast on the beach. The inhabitants of Tynemouth, and the neighbouring village of Cullercoats, which can be seen in the background, are said to have hurried away with the cargo of timber. It kept many a home warm that winter. The wreck was broken up on the beach, and most of the salvage was taken away. The boiler, however, had filled with sand and proved impossible to lift.

22. When the local Council permitted bathing-machines and a few refreshment booths on the beach, other recreations followed. The photograph, which probably dates from the 1890s, shows the beach black with tourists, and there is plenty to occupy them. Dominating the scene, as always, is the Plaza. Clustered on the beach are ranks of bathing-machines, fronted by a number of booths selling teas and souvenirs. There are several rows of swing-boats, or 'Shuggy-shoes', as they are known locally. The wooden horses on the cart perhaps belong to the roundabout, which is described as the latest novelty. A large placard advertises the Switchback, which stood in front of the Plaza.

23. Early in the nineteenth century the Fry and Linkleter families were involved in the provision of
bathing facilities, lodgings and refreshments. The Frys were already established in Prior's Haven when
James Linkleter married their daughter, Sarah, in 1841. She had her own fleet of bathing-machines,
which her husband, an active inventor, redesigned when they moved to the Long Sands in the 1850s.
The North Pier works must have affected their trade there. Both families had stalls in the line of refreshment booths, to the left, and shared responsibility for the safety of bathers. In the foreground is
the Aerial Flight, a Linkleter venture. One small boy can be seen sliding down the steel cables, and
another is about to launch himself from the platform.

S.3288   **GRAND PARADE. TYNEMOUTH.**

24. From the southern tower of the Plaza it was possible to see one of Tynemouth's open-air theatres. Sadly for the cast, none of the seats seem to be occupied. The audience are massed at the back, possibly to get away before the advent of the collecting-box, which was so necessary to the old pierrots, or concert parties. There used to be a number of these theatres. One was in Tynemouth Park, where a minstrel troupe was found to be charging for Corporation seats. At least one was built to the north of the Plaza, and to the south was the stage in this picture. Another, less permanent, was on the grass banks in the centre.

25. In 1907, Mister Graham, owner of the struggling Tynemouth Palace, attempted to control his competition by offering to take over the concert party theatre, and move it to the north. He intended that it be re-erected between the Public Shelter, which had been the skating rink, and the Palace. The Council, however, refused, and leased the stage to another concert party manager. Local residents remember that in later years this stage was erected on Mister Graham's site. In this show two women are giving an exhibition of boxing. The theatre was only short-lived, being blown down in a gale.

The Pierrots, Tynemouth

26. William Hunter, having had a successful season with his pierrot troupe at Tynemouth in 1905, sought to return in the following year. At first the Council tried to take a lease on the field at the south of Tynemouth Park, to house his show, but the Duke of Northumberland's agent refused to allow the tenant to sub-let. Accordingly the Borough Surveyor had a small, but sturdy, stage put up, just to the south of the Palace, much to the chagrin of its owner. There were also complaints that members of the cast were pursuing visitors into the nearby shelter, seeking contributions. The following seasons were disastrous, and the stage was demolished at the end of 1910.

WIL HUNTER'S TYNEMOUTH PIERROTS 1907

27. At the turn of the century the local Council decided that there should be no pierrots on the sea-banks, but minstrel troupes were encouraged to play in Tynemouth Park bandstand. Later a platform was built for them in an enclosed tennis court. This stage was demolished at the end of 1904, and in the summer of 1905 William Hunter's Pierrots had a stand on the sea-banks, at the bottom of Percy Park Road. He must have impressed the Councillors, because for the 1906 season they built the stage for him next to the Plaza. Following a bad season in 1908, Will Hunter refused to lease the stage again, unless the Council provided a canvas cover. His successor lost heavily on the 1909 season.

The Bathing Pool, Tynemouth. (6444)

28. From Sharpness Point the photographer has captured many of the sea-side amusements available at Tynemouth in the mid-1920s. As ever, the Plaza dominates the sky-line. The picture would have been taken at about the time its name was changed from Tynemouth Palace. On the bankside to the left is the wood and canvas theatre which stood at the bottom of Percy Park Road. A number of troupes played there, perhaps the best remembered locally being that of Victor Merrow, in 1933. Brown and Merrow were the proprietors of the Howard Hall cinema in nearby North Shields. In the foreground is the Open Air Pool, seen not long after it opened in 1925.

29. In 1909, following a number of deaths whilst bathing from the Long Sands, the Coroner urged the building of a swimming pool. A number of suggestions were made over the years, but plans for the Open Air Pool were not passed until 1923. The poor structure of the rock at Sharpness Point delayed completion, but the baths were opened on 30th May 1925. As originally planned, there were no dressing rooms or other facilities provided, and the Council hired tents, which were erected on the terraces. The Open Air Pool was an immediate success, leading the Council to build the Pavilion, to the right, which opened on 2nd July 1927.

WRECK AT TYNEMOUTH AP 15th 07.

30. On 15th April 1907, the wreck of a small sailing vessel came ashore at Sharpness Point. It was discovered to be the schooner 'Onward', which had been drifting for nearly a month. Outward bound from Littleferry to Sunderland, with a cargo of timber, she had been caught in a gale on 17th March. The ship was making water fast when she fell in with the steam trawler 'Cleon', which was on trials and making for Blyth. On the morning of the 18th they were off Blyth, with the tug 'Livingstone' in attendance, when 'Onward' turned turtle and had to be abandoned.

31. Early in 1919, the Secretary of the Local War Savings Committee received a letter offering the Borough a tank, in recognition of their efforts during the Great War. It was accepted, and a site prepared for it near the Grand Hotel, on Sharpness Point. A female tank, number 2663, newly returned from Flanders, arrived at Tynemouth Station on 21st June 1919. The crew drove it down Percy Park Road to the Grand Parade, where the acceptance ceremony was held. The Town Clerk requested the addition of two captured field guns, and these trophies were despatched in September, to stand alongside the tank. Seen at first as patriotic trophies, they came to be regarded as eyesores and were removed in 1923. The tank was sold for £20.

32. A tram is travelling along Percy Park Road, near the junction with Warkworth Terrace. The vehicle in the picture belonged to the Tynemouth and District Electric Traction Company, whose trams ran between North Shields and Whitley Bay, from 1901 to 1931. The houses in the background were all to be known as Warkworth Terrace when the Duke of Northumberland was having the ground laid out for builders, in 1868. The terrace should have continued to the left, and around the far corner, but was not completed until fairly recently. When the picture was taken, the house to the left was occupied by J.A. Williamson, a founder member of the Percy Park Rugby Football Club.

33. Towards the end of the 1860s, the Duke of Northumberland began plans for laying out the fields to the north of Tynemouth Village, for the building of terraces of new housing. The northernmost was Percy Park, taking its name from the family name of the Dukes of Northumberland. The first four houses were built at the seaward end of Percy Park, between 1868 and 1870, and the rest followed piecemeal throughout the 1870s. The triangular ground between Percy Park and Percy Park Road was urged on the Council, by Tynemouth Recreation Association, as an alternative to Tynemouth Park. Exhibitions and entertainments were held there over the years, and between times the land was fenced off for grazing cattle.

34. Percy Park is Tynemouth's oldest surviving Rugby Union football club. One of the first four **houses** in Percy Park was occupied by John Stanley Mitcalfe, and his nephew, John Stanley Todd. Mister Todd was a keen sportsman, and soon set about forming a local rugby club. They first played on a field by Percy Park in 1872. The team played on a number of other fields in later years, one of which might have brought their long career to a premature end. The Cycling Track ground in North Shields was built over an old colliery, which collapsed, shortly after the end of a match in the 1880s. The team was photographed in 1881, outside the Volunteer Life Brigade Watch House. Seated at the front, with a handlebar moustache, is J. Stanley Todd.

35. The standards for the tram wires, every few yards along Percy Park Road, would have been quite a recent feature at the time the photograph was taken. The tramway ran on this route, from North Shields to the Grand Parade, in 1879. It began as a horse-tram, which was replaced by a company using small steam engines to pull the carriages. The firm was taken over in 1899 by British Electric Traction, who set up a local subsidiary and built an extended line, which opened in 1901. To the right is William R. Hughson's newsagent's shop, which he ran from the mid-1890s, to about 1910. T.O. Mawson, the chemist, had the corner shop.

GRAND HOTEL. TYNEMOUTH 1189

36. One of the most luxurious hotels in the district, the Grand, opened at the northern end of Percy Gardens in the late 1870s. In its early days it saw a number of managers, but possibly the best-known locally was Thomas Tickle. He was associated with the hotel throughout the 1890s, and at one time ran both the Grand, and the Bath Hotel. He died in the Grand Hotel in 1900, whilst playing billiards with one of the Tynemouth Park pierrots. His widow continued as manageress for another decade. The photograph was probably taken early in the Great War, during which the building was occupied by troops. When they left, the hotel was in such a poor condition that it had to be completely refurbished. It did not re-open until 1922.

Percy Gardens. *Tynemouth*.

37. In 1868, the Duke of Northumberland's office produced ground plans for the building of terraces of large new houses on his Tynemouth estate. One of the showpieces of the development was to be a crescent of elegant homes overlooking the Short Sands and Tynemouth Priory. To emphasise its exclusive nature, it was to have a private road, and a railed communal garden on the seaward side. Although the ground plan was approved and laid out in the 1860s, the construction was left to individual owners and builders. Percy Gardens was erected in groups of one to four houses throughout the 1870s, and was still unfinished by the end of the decade.

38. No provision was made in the plans to give gardens to the houses in Percy Gardens. Instead, the small park on the cliff road was to be held in common by all the residents. By the time some dozen or more families were in occupation, it was decided to employ a gardener, and to this end application was made to the local Council for permission to build a lodge close to the southern gate. The plans were approved in April 1872. Surrounding the gardens are the original railings, which were removed as part of a salvage drive during the Second World War. Someone has drawn on the original photograph the extent of the damage to the road in the landslip of 1913.

39. **A name long associated with the gardener's lodge at Percy Gardens was that of John Grieve. He** spent much of his early life in Yorkshire, before moving to Tyneside in the mid-1870s. Mister Grieve was the gardener at Percy Gardens for over thirty years, being followed by Harold Teasdale, and later by Peter Redpath. For the photograph, the lodge seems to have been decorated not merely with potted plants, but also with greenery tied to the gutters and porch. From the great numbers of conifers the gardener might almost be preparing for Christmas. Alternatively, these could be part of the decorations for the visit of the Prince of Wales, in 1884.

40. Percy Bay, known more recently as King Edward's Bay, has always been called the Short Sands by local residents. At one time it had a rock-strewn shore. A guide book of 1825 recorded that a great storm a few years previously, had carried in an immense amount of sand, converting the bay into an instant bathing beach for ladies. Rocks began to appear once more however, as the cliffs around the bay crumbled. By the turn of the century there were those who wondered if the magnificent view from Percy Gardens was any compensation for the prospect of suddenly seeing it from the beach. The building of Percy Gardens did not proceed smoothly. At least one builder went into liquidation in 1876, and sites 7 to 13 were unoccupied until recent years.

41. Sharpness Point and the Short Sands had been subject to landslips for as long as anyone could remember, but when a large quantity of rock fell from the north side of Percy Bay in September 1900, the Borough Surveyor recommended that the cliffs be shored up. In the event, nothing was done until 1913. Early in the year cracks were noted in the road at Sea Banks, and a watchman was set to warn of any slippage. Some twenty yards of road fell into the bay at about eight o'clock on 27th January, and more was obviously about to follow. A resident wrote to the local newspaper, incensed at the Council, for making a number of labourers work on the endangered road, rescuing 5 or 6 shillings worth of iron railings.

THE LANDSLIP. TYNEMOUTH. 1185.

42. Controversy raged in the local press following the landslip. The Borough Surveyor pointed out that he had warned of it in 1900, and suggested a remedy. Others claimed he was responsible for the fall, by relaying an old sewer that could not be made watertight. The landslip lay along the sewer, and a heavy steam roller had been used on the trench only a few days before. One correspondent stated that the sewer was obviously the only cause, and dismissed claims that sea-erosion, shale beds and natural springs were responsible – there was nothing wrong with the cliffs. A large quantity of rock promptly fell out of the south side of the bay, crushing a refreshment hut on the beach. The gap in the road eventually widened to some 80 yards.

KING EDWARDS BAY AND PROMENADE, TYNEMOUTH (2)

43. There were those who held that the Sea Banks should be left to collapse as they would, after the 1913 landslip. Towards the end of the year, however, a special committee was set up to plan the rebuilding of the road. Work began in the middle of 1914, and the new road, supported by reinforced concrete pillars, opened early in 1915. Plans for further works were cancelled due to restrictions on borrowing. During the Depression, plans were sought to provide temporary work for the unemployed. On condition that at least half the workers were ex-servicemen, a grant was paid for the construction of the Lower Promenade. It was begun in 1927, but not formally opened until 1931.

44. Before the Duke's estate at Tynemouth was built up, it was possible to see for miles to the north, from the castle. In those days the village ended on the site of Lovaine Row, which was part of the development of the 1870s. On the site of the gardener's cottage in Percy Gardens, there were two buildings, known as East Houses. The fairly gently sloping land fell away sharply into King Edward's Bay at the end of the wall in the foreground. This made the cliff-side cottages something of a curiosity to visitors, as mass tourism grew in Tynemouth. The cottagers were quick to take advantage, by opening refreshment rooms.

45. With plenty of open space around the village, it must have been a great source of wonder to nineteenth century tourists that people would choose to perch their homes in such a precarious position. The original cottages grew, and were added to in stone, brick and wood, throughout the century. In addition to being the homes of local artisans, those cottages at street level became refreshment rooms. In the background is East Street, with the old Priory Inn to the left. The Council decided to widen the road in 1918, but the scheme was delayed repeatedly. In 1934 the cottages were demolished and the banks landscaped.

46. Long before tourists came to admire Tynemouth's 'noble ruins', medieval pilgrims travelled to the Priory in search of miracles. The church was founded in the seventh century on Pen-bal-crag – 'the head of the rampart on the rock'. Beyond the headland is the mouth of the Tyne, making the monastery an obvious place for a lighthouse. A turret on the church became a light-tower in 1581, but it collapsed in 1659. The Governor of the Castle built a new one in 1664, which was taken down and rebuilt as seen in the distance, in 1775. The light continued to burn until 1898, when it was replaced by that on St. Mary's Island. Sea View Cottage was run by William Mann Bell, between 1895 and 1910.

SEA BANKS TYNEMOUTH

47. Lancaster's Café and Thomason's Refreshment Rooms, seen about 1908, were new names for old-established businesses. One of the original houses on the cliff-side was Rock Cottage, which was rebuilt in 1861. The Lupton family ran it as a refreshment room from the middle of the century. Mary Lupton was followed by her son James, and his wife Catherine. Although Catherine had married Samuel Kelly by 1871, the building was known as Lupton's Refreshment Rooms until about 1895. William Thomason, who had premises in Front Street, took it over. Lancaster's Café, on the corner of Percy Street, was a successor to the Temperance Hotel, run by the Bell sisters since the 1870s. Their mother, Isabella, was a lodging house keeper before them.

OPENING OF TYNEMOUTH
READING ROOM
BY ROLAND PHILIPSON ESQR
SEP 6 06

48. Following the closure of a branch library, the people of the village felt a sense of loss. Eventually a group organised the setting up of a Men's Reading room for Tynemouth residents. The president of the institution was the Reverend Mister Samuel Pearson, a Congregational minister. One of their prime movers, and principal benefactors, was a local civil engineer, Mister Roland Philipson. The Reading Room was at 2 Middle Street, and the opening ceremony was performed by Mister Philipson on 6th September 1906. The members having given of their labours, he offered to supply them with 'one hundred of the best books that could be got'.

49. A picture of East Street in 1860 was re-issued on a number of occasions, for the sake of its period charm. From early in the nineteenth century, until his death in 1876, Ralph Pigg was a grocer in the village, and also its first postmaster. The building with the large lamp over the door is the old Gibraltar Rock Inn, which at this time would have been run by Matthew Bell. On the white building is a signboard which proclaims it to be the Visitors' Rest, otherwise John Marshall's Tea and Coffee Rooms. The Priory Inn of those days was a very small affair, and appears, almost tucked out of sight, at the end of the Visitors' Rest.

50. From being the small bar-room in the centre of the picture, the Priory Inn grew to take over the cottage next door, by the turn of the century. During much of this time Thomas Mothersdale was the licensee. The white-painted frontage represents the old Visitors' Rest tea rooms and another cottage, which together became Dux Ferguson's Café. Another of Mister Ferguson's activities was that of dancing teacher. The present Gibraltar Rock Restaurant takes part of the sites of Ferguson's Café and the original inn of that name, to the right. On the left, at 1 Middle Street, is George Grey's Dial House Temperance Hotel.

TYNEMOUTH PRIORY CHURCH IN 1450   No. 162

51. When King Oswin of Deira was murdered in the year 651, he was buried at a small church at Tynemouth, where he came to be revered as a saint. From the year 800 onwards there were two centuries of Danish raids, which led to the monastery of Tynemouth being abandoned in 1008. The saint's last resting place was forgotten for almost sixty years. Following a dream, in which Saint Oswin called upon him to raise his relics to a position of dignity, a novice monk called Edmund rediscovered the tomb on 11th March 1065. In time this event lead to the re-establishment of the Priory at Tynemouth, and its rise to prosperity.

TYNEMOUTH PRIORY

52. Despite the seemingly miraculous finding of the relics of Saint Oswin, in 1065, the upheavals of the Norman invasion delayed the growth of a new monastery at Tynemouth. Earl Waltheof did give it to the monks of Jarrow, but it was removed from their care and given into the keeping of the Benedictine Priory at St. Albans by Robert de Mowbray, Earl of Northumberland. The new order of monks began to arrive in 1090. The monastery at Tynemouth grew to be a substantial building in their hands, in spite of the fact that Tynemouth's strategic importance caused the Priory to become part of a fortress, which was embroiled from time to time in rebellion and wars with the Scots.

53. According to a letter written by one of the medieval monks: 'The church is of a wondrous beauty. It has been lately completed. Within it lies the body of the blessed martyr Oswin in a silver shrine, magnificently embellished with gold and jewels. He protects the murderers, thieves and seditious persons who fly to him, and commutes their punishment to exile. He heals those whom no physician can cure.' The eastern end of the nave, in a thirteenth century addition to the Norman church, is the best preserved portion of the edifice. The door below the centre window leads to the Percy Chantry.

Lady Chapel, Tynemouth Priory

216

54. The only part of the old Priory to have remained almost intact is the Percy Chantry, at the extreme east end of the nave, behind the altar. It is believed to have been built in the middle of the fifteenth century, when the monastery was at the height of its powers. The vaulting of the roof is composed of intersecting ribs, with thirty-two sculptured bosses. From the presence of Percy and Delaval heraldry carved in the stone it is believed that this was built as a chantry for the souls of the Percys. During the military occupation of the Priory, this room was converted into a gunpowder store. This seems to have preserved it from further damage.

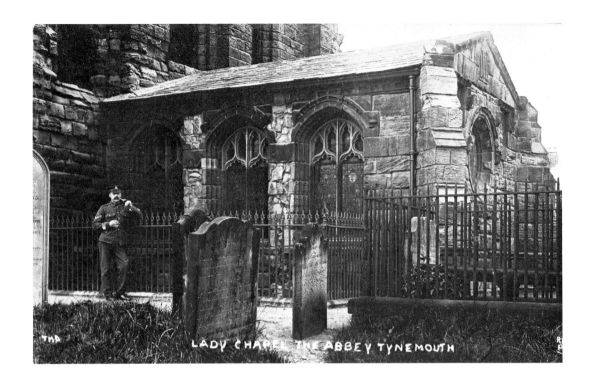

LADY CHAPEL THE ABBEY TYNEMOUTH

55. The Percy Chantry has occasionally been referred to as the Lady Chapel, which no longer exists. From the Civil War onwards, the military authorities gradually sought to exclude the public from the castle grounds, and demolished much of the Priory. One Governor of the Castle even took to charging parishioners for the use of the graveyard. In 1846 William Sidney Gibson published a two-volume history of the monastery that re-awakened the public interest. Eventually the chantry was restored, and one of the new stained glass windows commemorates Mister Gibson's efforts to that end.

56. From being a great house in the fifteenth century, Tynemouth Priory was so reduced by the border wars, and military demands on its resources, that by the time of the Dissolution, in 1539, there were only the Prior, fifteen monks, and three novices left. Under Henry VIII, the Priory became a Royal castle for the defence of the Tyne. Areas where once monks and pilgrims prayed were given over to stabling and storage. On the south side a large public house, the Ordnance Arms, was built. Those buildings which did not collapse through neglect began to be demolished to build barns and barracks.

THE CASTLE, TYNEMOUTH.   217886.

57. Although founded as a religious house, Tynemouth Priory, of necessity became a fortress in medieval times. Licence to crenellate the walls was granted as early as 1296. Much of the gatehouse was built towards the end of the fourteenth century, and the curtain walls date from the reign of Elizabeth I. Despite the decay of later years, many thought the castle to be a noble and romantic sight. Antiquarians were disgusted, therefore, when the War Office built a superstructure, largely of brick, on top of the old walls, in about 1783. Many rejoiced when it caught fire in 1936, and had to be demolished.

58. The Norman church, in the background, had an eastern extension built in the early English style, in the thirteenth century. As pilgrims began to interfere with the devotions of the monks, the church was divided in 1220. The western portion was given over to the use of the parish. The castle fell to Parliamentary troops in 1644, and they seem to have so neglected the fabric of the church that in 1659 the roof fell in, killing a number of them. From the middle of the nineteenth century, agitation grew to restore what was left of the Priory to public access. The site passed into the care of the Office of Works in 1904; a number of restoration and excavation projects have been carried on since then.

59. One preserved stone in the Priory grounds was brought from a nearby farm in 1936. The Monk's Stone, so the legend has it, marked the boundary of the ecclesiastical lands, beyond which all were safe from civil authority. One day, a monk from the Priory went to beg food at Earl Delaval's hall. Being refused, he stole a pig's head, roasting for the lord's supper. When Earl Delaval found out, he pursued the monk, overtaking him at the stone marker. This notwithstanding, he beat the monk so severely that he died within a year and a day. As penance he gave up his manor of Elswick to the Priory. On the stone was carved the line: 'O horor, to kill a man for a pigge's hede.'

60. Captain Casimir Thomas Gomoszynski, in everyday life the Tynemouth Borough Surveyor, was also a member of Tynemouth Artillery Volunteers. In 1859, at a time when war with Napoleon III was feared, Tynemouth set up the first Volunteer Artillery Corps, a fact of which the local people were very proud. By 1880 they were six batteries strong, and the senior Volunteer Corps on the Army List. Proposals to amalgamate them with a Newcastle Corps provoked popular indignation, and following petitions to the Secretary of State for War, they retained their position. The Volunteers became Tynemouth Royal Garrison Artillery, as part of the Territorial Army, in 1907, and disbanded in 1959.

61. The lawns now surrounding the Priory give little hint of the extent to which the military authorities took over the grounds. To the left are the barracks, storerooms and hospital, together with the light-house, built in 1775. An earlier tower on the site used stone from the monastery buildings. Towards the turn of the century the light was replaced by others at St. Mary's Island and the North Pier. To the right is the large magazine mound, for which the cloister buildings were destroyed between 1863 and 1865. In the distance is the North Pier, which was begun in the middle of the nineteenth century, but not completed by the time the photograph was taken, towards the end of the century.

The Black Middens, North Shields

62. For centuries the Tyne was a treacherous river to enter. Strong currents along the coast and a narrow, winding entrance to the harbour, brought many ships to grief. Even in the days of steam, ships were lost on the Black Middens rocks, on the north bank of the Tyne, or on the Herd Sands to the south. When the Tyne Improvement Commission was set up in 1850, one of its priorities was the creation of a harbour of refuge at the mouth of the river. This was a massive engineering project for its time, and took over fifty years to complete.

WRECK AT TYNEMOUTH. Geo.

63. Shortly after ten o'clock on 20th October 1894, a ship was sighted labouring off the harbour entrance. She was the brigantine 'Fame', of Drogheda, on passage from Llanelly to West Hartlepool carrying burnt ore. A huge sea washed her behind the North Pier, where she was trapped by the waves. The Volunteer Life Brigade, finding themselves unable to summon help, prepared to rescue the crew alone. As soon as the ship grounded, they fired rocket lines over her, one catching in the mainmast and setting it alight. Within fifteen minutes all the crew of six were rescued by breeches buoy.

64. 'Rupert', a Faversham brigantine, under the command of Captain Burdon, was sailing from Sunderland to Ramsgate when she was forced to run before a hurricane from the safety of Shields Harbour. On Christmas Eve 1895, she was seen off Souter Point light, down at the stern with water in the hold. At Shields Bar she turned broadside on to the gale, and began to suffer damage. Whilst apparently trying to run into the Haven, she was swept onto the Black Middens and dismasted. The crew, who had taken to the rigging, were all lost in a few minutes, and the vessel quickly broke up.

65. As originally conceived, both the North and South Piers, at the mouth of the Tyne, were to be curved. A Government grant led the Tyne Improvement Commissioners to carry the piers out to thirty feet of water. The contract was let in 1855, but in 1862, following disputes with the contractor, the Commissioners took over the works for themselves. Even with the advice of their own engineer, and that of others, the piers extended seawards very slowly. The finishing touches were being put to the North Pier in 1895, when the photograph was taken from Prior's Haven. A small commercial jetty is seen to the right, below Spanish Battery.

66. Early in its life, the half-mile length of the North Pier became an important tourist attraction. Promenading the upper deck, in particular, was very popular at the turn of the century. It was, perhaps, inevitable that such a potential market should attract the attention of the river's ferry and pleasure boat operators. Trippers were offered the choice of cruises along the Northumbrian coast or journies up the river, to Newcastle. When the photograph was taken, work was under way in the background removing the end of the pier.

"*Doon the river to Tinmuth,*" on a *Tyne Ferry Steamer.*

HALF HOUR SAILINGS
FROM QUAYSIDE.

FARES { 6D. SINGLE.
9D. RETURN.

Printed and Published by ANDREW REID & CO., Ltd., 50, Grey Street, Newcastle-on-Tyne.

67. The Tyne General Ferry Company was given to issuing postcards illustrating the views on the River Tyne, and advertising its own services. Beginning as the Tyne Passenger Boat Service in 1859, they became the Tyne General Ferry Company in 1862. Over the years they had twenty-one boats, operating a zig-zag route along the river, between Newcastle Quayside and Tynemouth North Pier. In addition, their vessel 'Siren' toured the North-East coast. The company took its main revenue from the carriage of workmen to the shipyards and factories. As local tram services grew, the ferries could not compete, and the company went out of business in 1908.

68. Whilst not unprecedented, the building of the harbour of refuge for the Tyne was a huge task in its day. The work was bedevilled by delays and upsets caused by lack of knowledge as to how materials might behave in these conditions. In 1867 a quantity of the rubble foundation was pulled out of the pier by the sea. From the winter of 1893 many of the concrete blocks were found to be moving. The sinking of the ship 'Roxana', loaded with concrete, in 1896, failed to give sufficient protection to the pier, which began to break up in the winter of 1897.

69. Following the opening up of a one hundred yard wide gap in the North Pier, in January 1897, a contract was let to Sir John Jackson in October 1898, to build a new, straight pier. The new section was to be added from approximately half-way along the old curved pier. Concrete blocks, faced with stone, were constructed in Prior's Haven and carried out along the pier to be set in place by giant cranes. In the photograpfh a Titan crane is erecting a Goliath crane on gantries. It was decided to leave the old pier in position for as long as possible, in order to provide a breakwater whilst building the new pier.

Tynemouth Pier

70. Taken shortly after it was completed, the photograph shows the new North Pier, as seen from Prior's Haven. With modern techniques, and the shelter provided by the ruins of the old pier, it was possible to effect the junction of the old and new piers by the summer of 1906. The ruins were largely cleared away during 1907. The end of the new pier was finished early in 1907, but the old lighthouse was allowed to stand until the new one was built. It was commissioned in 1908, and the old light was demolished by the end of the year. Swelling of the mortar canted the upper works, and delayed completion of the pier until 1909.

71. The Tyne has seen many hundreds of ships pass through the piers, but one of the most famous and best loved was the Cunard liner 'Mauretania'. She was laid down at the Swan, Hunter and Wigham Richardson shipyard, Wallsend, in 1905, and launched in September 1906. At the time she was the biggest ship ever built, and one of the fastest. 'Mauretania' went into service in 1907, and for twenty-two years held the speed record for Atlantic crossings, only losing it to the new German liner 'Bremen' in 1929. Here she is seen returning from her trials, passing the North Pier in the short period when it had two lighthouses.

72. Early in the afternoon of 5th September 1903, thirteen lifeboats were towed into Prior's Haven. They were watched by thick crowds on the North Pier, and many others on the beach and at the Spanish Battery. The occasion was Lifeboat Saturday, a fund-raising event for the Royal National Lifeboat Institution. Amongst the boats present was the 'Willie Wouldhave', from South Shields, which commemorated the North Shields native who invented the first self-righting lifeboat, in 1789. The organisers must have been sadly disappointed, as the estimated 100,000 spectators contributed just £89 13s. 6d.

The Pier Tynemouth

73. At the beginning of the nineteenth century Tynemouth's principal bathing beach was at Prior's Haven. It was particularly attractive to those who spent most of the year in the smoke and grime of the Tyneside towns. In his description of northern spas, published in 1841, Doctor A.B. Granville stated that he had never seen anything less inviting, it being a confined space, full of sharp rocks, with a few straggling bathing-machines and a small old bath house. Many, however, preferred the shelter offered by the cliffs, even before the pier was built. Even the years of disturbance caused by the pier did not deter visitors. The railway from Tynemouth goods yard continued long after the pier was completed.

74. *Away down yonder on the beach, The village boatman stands; The boatman a jokey man is he, With lots of curious yarns; For such like stories suit the folk That loiter on the sands. Week in, week out, from morn till night, He paces to and fro; You can hear him ask the trippers, If they'll kindly take a row.* 'The Village Boatman' was dedicated to Thomas Ferguson, pictured in 1896, in Prior's Haven. He was a dredger master for the Tyne Improvement Commission, but gave up the work for pleasure boating. Mister Ferguson was well-known on the sands as a teller of sea stories, and was greatly missed after his death in 1901.

75. In the 1890s Prior's Haven had taken on a crowded look. The building with the tall chimney was the Sea Water Bath, which existed from 1807 to about 1894, to provide visitors with hot, cold, and shower baths, without the necessity of entering the sea. Originally water was drawn from the bay by means of a horse-mill. For many years it was associated with the Bath Hotel, Front Street. The building with a flagstaff was the boathouse of the Tynemouth Rowing Club, established in 1867. The slip-way leads to the lifeboat house, to which a small mortuary for those found drowned, was added in 1864. The first National Lifeboat Institution craft arrived there in 1862. In the background is a gantry for the pier works blockyard.

76. Its sheltered position between the castle and the Spanish Battery has always made Prior's Haven a favoured pleasure beach. The lawns in the background held the Sea Water Baths until the 1890s, and for those who preferred the water in its natural state, there were bathing-machines and covered boats. For many years the Fry family dominated the sea-bathing and pleasure boat trade in the Haven, but in the mid-1860s a group of local gentlemen decided to provide their own craft. The Tynemouth Rowing Club was formed, and held its first competitions in August 1867. At the time the boathouse, a cruciform building to the left, was still being built.

77. Tynemouth Amateur Swimming Club had their photograph taken during the celebrations of Queen Victoria's Diamond Jubilee, on 22nd June 1897. The club was formed in 1875 to promote the 'science and art of natation'. It was claimed that they had an advantage over other swimming clubs, in the membership of P.J. Messent, the Engineer to the Tyne Improvement Commission. At first they were allowed to change in one of the North Pier arches, and later their hut was built on the pier, giving easy access to safe water. Over the years the Club's swimming masters taught many hundreds of Tyneside children.

78. The winning water polo teams of the Tynemouth Amateur Swimming Club sat amongst the sea-weed and posed for W.W. Fry on 27th August 1895. John William Moore, seated at the back, wearing a dark moustache, was one of the Club's earliest swimming masters. He had a large printing works in North Shields, but in his spare time he was tireless in his efforts to encourage young people to learn how to swim. At first, lessons were held from the dressing rooms at the foot of the North Pier, far enough down Prior's Haven to have shallow water outside the door. In 1907 the Club took over a salt water reservoir in North Shields, and Mister Moore transferred the lessons there.

79. In the 1820s Pier Road was a coach road from Tynemouth Village to the sea-water baths in Prior's Haven. It was owned by Mister Hutchinson and Miss Spurrier, of the Bath Hotel in Front Street. Above and to the right, is the brick office block built over the original castle gateshouse, and despised by antiquarians since its construction in about 1783. It was removed after catching fire in 1936. It has been said that the castle moat is not as originally built, it having been enlarged by the first contractor on the North Pier, whilst he was looking for suitable building stone.

80. In the foreground are the timbers on the concrete jetty at the North Pier, at which the Tyne General Ferry boats used to tie up. On this occasion their ferry appears to have called at the long jetty from Spanish Battery field, which existed during the 1890s. The skyline is instantly recognisable, and yet there are differences to the modern scene. Admiral Collingwood's monument towers above everything, and is the most significant landmark in the area. In the centre, the Tynemouth Volunteer Life Brigade watch house is flying a great many signal flags. When the photograph was taken, only one of the two towers existed, and even that was later raised in height.

81. From the old Bath Hotel, at Bath Terrace, it was possible to watch the reconstruction of the North
Pier, between 1898 and 1909. In earlier days the smoke from the sea-water baths, with which the hotel
was associated, would have been visible. At the far side of Prior's Park, the low-lying area known as
the Howlings was filled with materials for the building of the pier. The three gantries straddled railway
lines from Tynemouth Station. As always, Collingwood's Monument dominated the scene, and had
done since 1845. To its left is the wooden building used by the Volunteer Life Brigade since 1887. The
tower was higher after 1905.

82. The distant view of the lighthouse at Tynemouth castle identifies the photograph as a south-west view of Spanish Battery, taken before 1898. When the Priory was dissolved in 1539 the surrounding fortifications were in a state of considerable disrepair. Plans were laid to turn the castle into a strong fortress for the defence of the Tyne. Early in 1545 one thousand impressed workmen began reinforcing the walls, and building a new curtain wall to cover the harbour entrance. In April of that year 1,300 Spanish mercenaries were landed at Newcastle, and a party of them was sent to man the new guns, hence – Spanish Battery.

83. Spanish Battery, built under instructions from the Privy Council and Sir Richard Lee, was a small fortress of low stone walls. In active service it would have been difficult to observe from the sea. Shortly before the English Civil War, in 1643, the fortifications were strengthened, with the aid of public subscriptions. The stone walls had a brick superstructure raised upon them. The embrasures covering the river are hidden behind the barracks and storerooms. In later years, from the 1880s, the battery was used to train Volunteer Corps, including the Submarine Miners, known locally as 'Mussel Shifters', from the effects of their mines on the river. In recent years the area became a car park.

Admiral Collingwood Memorial, Tynemouth. 408

84. Cuthbert Collingwood was born in Newcastle in 1748, the son of a merchant, and member of a family with extensive local land holdings. He went to sea with the Royal Navy in 1761, and rose to be Admiral Lord Collingwood, second in command of the British fleet at the Battle of Trafalgar, in 1805. Following the battle he was at sea until his death in 1810. In 1838 the first move was made to create a local monument to him. John Gordon Lough was commissioned to sculpt the statue, which arrived at the riverside site on 19th August 1845; it was completed on the 30th. The guns came from his flagship 'Royal Sovereign', and were put up in 1849.

TRAFALGAR

TRAFALGAR DAY TYNEMOUTH OCT 21 1905.

85. Many subscribers withdrew their offers of help when it was decided to erect the monument at the coast rather than in Newcastle. The people of Tynemouth, however, were proud of the statue, and perhaps never more so than on the centenary of the Battle of Trafalgar. On 21st October 1905, a procession marched from the village to the cliffs. It was the first function for the Harbour Boroughs Companies of the Royal Naval Volunteers, but the boys of the training ship 'Wellesley' were old hands at the Trafalgar Day celebrations. The Coastguard and the Royal Garrison Artillery also participated, and members of the Collingwood family were in attendance. The Volunteer Life Brigade closed the proceedings with a rocket exercise.

86. The Tyne is essentially a commercial river, and has been one of the foremost ports in the country. For centuries Newcastle claimed the bulk of the trade on the river, but the ruins of Tynemouth Priory, in the distance, are a reminder that the city did not have things all their own way. As early as 1225 the Prior was encouraging fishermen to trade at the Pow Burn, the birthplace of North Shields. A fish quay built there in 1870 brought fleets from the length of the North-East coast. The sailing drifter, here, had come from Kirkcaldy. Paddle tugs towed the boats to the fishing grounds, and in later years were converted for trawling.

THE HARBOUR FRO

87. Spanish Battery and the searchlight emplacements below were never to claim the ships and lives that had been lost to the shallows they overlooked. Even with the completion of the piers, shortly before the photograph was taken, ships were swept onto the Black Middens. Once ashore it was always difficult to refloat the stranded vessels, and salvage work was dangerous. Even attempting rescues was extremely hazardous. The Royal National Lifeboat Institution boathouse, in the foreground, was erected at the Black Middens to allow an easier approach to shipwrecks.

88. Tynemouth Volunteer Life Brigade's watch house has stood on the cliffs near Spanish Battery since 1887, having replaced an earlier building nearby. The Brigade operates alongside the Coastguard in the saving of lives from shipwreck. Indeed, the stone-built houses were once the abode of Coastguardmen. From 1905 the tower on the watch house has had an extra storey, to house a searchlight. The organisation was founded at the end of 1864, following a series of wrecks at the mouth of the Tyne. The most notable was that of the steamer 'Stanley'. One of their principal tools was the rocket line and breeches buoy.

89. On 24th November 1864, the schooner 'Friendship' and the iron screw steamer 'Stanley' were driven onto the Black Middens in a gale. The lifeboats were unable to approach through the seas breaking over the rocks and 'Friendship' lost six of her crew. The Prior's Haven lifeboat was crippled and lost two of her crew. In the night 'Stanley' broke in two. The next morning it was found that 36 people had been killed in the wrecks. John Morrison, John F. Spence and Joseph Spence called a public meeting at which the first Volunteer Life Brigade in the country was set up. The Board of Trade provided aid, including the cart with the rescue equipment.

WRECK OF THE 'DIAMANTE', TYNEMOUTH. 1731. *Auty.*

90. The barque 'Diamant', of Sandfjord, was observed running before a gale on 26th March 1898. She got safely between the piers, only to have a heavy sea damage the wheel-house. Despite the efforts of the crew, her stern struck the Black Middens and 'Diamant' was driven round to lie caught fast on the rocks. In view of the weather, the Volunteer Life Brigade had been standing watch all night, and quickly made their way down the stricken vessel. The first rocket line fired fouled the ship's rigging, but the second succeeded, and the photographer recorded the rescue of the crew by breeches buoy.

91. Early in the morning of 8th December 1899, the steamship 'Craigneuk', of Leith, left from Smith's Dock at North Shields. She was going to sea on a voyage to Methil, in Scotland, where she would load cargo. As she was approaching the lighthouses, she took a shear and struck the North Pier. When going astern the propellor was fouled, causing the ship to drift onto the Battery Rocks. The Volunteer Life Brigade had been on duty during a gale in the night, and were soon on the scene. They put a rocket line over the ship, which can be seen fixed in the rigging, aft, and rescued all who were prepared to leave.

92. The Royal National Lifeboat Institution was still called the National Institution for the Preservation of Life from Shipwreck when they sent their first boat to Tynemouth. She was the 'Constance', and had a boathouse in Prior's Haven. In 1864, when the ships 'Stanley' and 'Friendship' were wrecked on the Black Middens, 'Constance' was rowed round the point to give assistance. Instead she was seriously damaged, and two of her crew were killed. As a consequence a second boat was installed on the Black Middens, below the Life Brigade watch house. She was the 'Pomfret and Goole', named for the towns which subscribed to her construction.

TYNEMOUTH LIFEBOAT.£85.

93. When the Black Middens lifeboat was introduced in 1865 the Prior's Haven boathouse became Number One Station. Number Two Station housed the 'Pomfret and Goole' between 1865 and 1872. She was followed by two craft, both called 'Forester', the name being taken from the Ancient Order of Foresters, whose gift they were. As the picture is believed to have been taken at the time of the wreck of the barque 'Diamant', in 1898, this must be the first 'Forester'. On that occasion she was not needed, as the crew were saved by the Tynemouth Volunteer Life Brigade.

94. Major H.E. Burton, of the Royal Engineers at Tynemouth, was actively interested in life saving. In 1905, when the Royal National Lifeboat Institution converted the Folkestone lifeboat 'J. McConnell Hussey' into their first motor-vessel, they sent it to Tynemouth, where Major Burton was a member of the local committee. Faced with the suspicions of the regular crew, he used volunteer soldiers until the lifeboatmen were convinced of the boat's worth. In 1914 he tended the engine of the 'Henry Vernon', from Tynemouth to Whitby, where pulling boats could not approach the hospital ship 'Rohilla'; a great vindication of the motor lifeboat.

95. Percy Square was originally built as a barracks in 1758. It consisted of four terraces built around a parade-ground, the whole overlooking the River Tyne and North Shields. After the Napoleonic Wars the area was sold to the Duke of Northumberland, who had the buildings converted into cottages. The parade-ground was railed and cultivated. In 1847 the north side was partially demolished for the railway cutting between North Shields and Tynemouth. The river side gradually fell victim to the erosion of the cliffs. The Sir James Knott Memorial Flats were opened on the site in 1938.

96. 'Wellesley' was an old naval sailing ship, converted for use as an industrial school and moored off North Shields. Boys unconvicted of crime, but in need of care, were accepted aboard. Between 1868 and 1914 hundreds of boys were trained for a life at sea and in the armed forces. The ship was well-known on Tyneside and further afield for the band, drill team and gun team which could be booked for fetes and other outdoor activities. Classes in seamanship were conducted aboard ship, but drilling with the seven-pounder gun was held in a field at Tynemouth, near the Master Mariners' Asylum. 'Wellesley' sank in 1914, and eventually the boys were taken to Blyth.

Master Mariners' Asylum, North Shields

Valentines Series

97. The Tyne Mariners' Benevolent Institution, on Tynemouth Road, near Knott's Flats, began as the Master Mariners' Asylum. In 1829 a friendly society was set up to provide pensions for retired ships' masters. The Duke of Northumberland gave the land for the building of the houses, and his statue in the grounds commemorates this act of generosity. The foundation stone was laid in 1837, and thirty-two, two-roomed houses had been built and paid for by 1840. The Tyne Mariners' Institute had been founded in 1897, to pay pensions to any old seamen. The two amalgamated in 1902, and became a charitable organisation.

98. North Shields and District Tramway Company introduced small steam locomotives to pull the carriages in 1882. In the 1890s the steam trams were run by North Shields and Tynemouth District Tramways Limited. The line was converted to electricity in 1901. The steam tram is on that part of Tynemouth Road known as Correction House Bank, running towards the lower gates of Northumberland Park. To the right, the road leads down to North Shields. Left of the engine is the magistrates' court attached to the House Of Correction, built in 1792. There were also a governor's house and fourteen cells. Behind the tram is the old established public house known as the Tynemouth Lodge inn, named after a local mansion.

NORTH SHIELDS PARK

99. 'Though the Corporation of Tynemouth did not accept my offer of the ground for a park in 1878 (and I might be justified in refusing to have anything more to do with the business) my wish is to consult the health and convenience of the inhabitants of Tynemouth to the exclusion of other considerations,' wrote the Duke of Northumberland to his agent in 1884. The ground referred to was Spital Dene, lying between Tynemouth and North Shields. It took its name from the medieval Saint Leonard's leper hospital, supposed to have stood at the northern end of Northumberland Park.

100. During the 1880s there was severe unemployment in the Tyneside shipbuilding industry. Alderman John Foster Spence saw an opportunity to provide work and an amenity for the Borough. He approached the Duke of Northumberland on his own initiative and persuaded him to donate ten acres of Spital Dene for use as a park, and encouraged the Council to accept. Work began on landscaping the Dene by December, 1884. Northumberland Park was opened in the following August. It became the custom to lay out one of the flower beds in honour of the current Mayor of the Borough of Tynemouth. In this case it was Councillor Jacob Daglish, elected in 1900.

THE PARK,
NORTH SHIELDS

101. A great deal of effort had gone into the making of Northumberland Park, and the townspeople were very proud of it. Over the years many have made contributions to its attractions. Wildfowl have graced its waters, including swans, from time to time. In 1897 a local Councillor offered an alligator for the lake. In 1893 a letter to the local newspaper heralded a new venture. A lady complained of an ugly hut which obscured her view of the bandstand and flower beds. It was to be one of a number of aviaries for exotic birds. Donations included an owl, a silver pheasant and a collection of parrots. As interest waned the largest house was demolished, in 1906, and the others in the 1920s.

Spittal Dene. North Shields. [5687]

1924

102. The northern end of Northumberland Park opens onto King Edward Road. To the left of the park railings is Saint Aidan's Home. The Church of England Society for Waifs and Strays built a home for girls in the neighbouring village of Cullercoats in 1895, and in 1901 took temporary premises in Whitley Bay, to house sixteen boys. In 1905 Saint Aidan's Home was built on the corner of King Edward Road and Mariners' Lane. At the other end of Mariners' Lane was the Master Mariners' Asylum. The road rises from Spital Dene, over the brow of the hill, and leads to Tynemouth Village. The photograph was taken after the road level was raised.

103. Spital Dene is a narrow valley leading the Pow Burn down to the River Tyne. Across it, King Edward Road leads to Tynemouth Village from North Shields. In earlier years the road was Cut Athwart, or, Cutty Throat Lane. In 1921, to give work to the unskilled unemployed, plans were laid to fill in the Dene at King Edward Road, and raise the road to its present level. The picture was taken in 1922, before the work was complete. In the background it is possible to see the embankment and bridge footings for the Blyth and Tyne Railway mineral line that ran alongside the Dene in the nineteenth century.

S 3297   HOLY SAVIOUR'S CHURCH, TYNEMOUTH.

104. Holy Saviour's Church was begun in 1838, and opened in 1841 as a chapel of ease to Christ Church, North Shields. When the old parish was divided in 1861, the chapel became the parish church of the Parish of Tynemouth Priory. The spire eventually began to list to one side, an occurrence blamed on the vibrations caused by firing heavy guns at Tynemouth Castle. After many years it was removed in 1957. Carved on the wall around the church is a heart and the inititals M.M., said to be the work of Samuel Emery, whilst waiting for Mary Ann Marshall, whom he murdered in a jealous rage, when they met there on 23rd July 1894.

105. Henry McQueen, of the Tynemouth Constabulary, was promoted to the rank of Inspector after his work on the murder of Mary Ann Marshall. Private Samuel George Emery, late of Tynemouth Castle, heard that his sweetheart was unfaithful. After writing accusing letters, he deserted, and lured her to a meeting at Holy Saviour's Church, where he killed her. He escaped the onlookers, but during the night was arrested in the street by Inspector McKenzie and Sergeant McQueen. The Sergeant found fragments of a letter in a ditch, which were vital evidence at the trial. At the age of 68, whilst at his bungalow on the Long Sands, he rescued his son from the sea. He was awarded one of the rare Tynemouth Trust Medals.

Front Street, Tynemouth.

1188.

106. Until the second half of the nineteenth century most of Tynemouth Village clustered around the broad sweep of Front Street. When Holy Saviour's Church, in the distance, was first erected, it stood alone in fields outside the village. Many have admired the simple but elegant eighteenth and early nineteenth century houses which front the street, although this appreciation has not been universal. Doctor Granville, in his 1841 guide to northern spas, dismissed Tynemouth's character as being that of ugliness, with the aspect of poverty to boot; worse even than North and South Shields.

FRONT ST. TYNEMOUTH

107. Manor Road, Tynemouth, takes its name from Manor House, the gate to which was on the road off to the right. On the left of Manor Road, with someone standing in the doorway, is Manor Cottage. Over the door is carved a crescent moon, the badge of the Percy family. There are those who remember that this was the manor office, where rents for town and beach properties were paid to the Duke of Northumberland's agent, Mister A. Ireland Wright. In the distance, the Co-operative Society store can be seen. It was opened in 1904, and the postcard was posted in January 1907.

Huntington Place, Tynemouth

108. Seen from the approach to Tynemouth Station, at some time before the postmarked date of 1917, the village green naturally does not contain the large memorial to the fallen of the First and Second World Wars. At the easternmost end of the green is the Boer War memorial, put up in 1903. Huntington Place stands to the right, with the large stone portico of Tynemouth House School most prominent along its length. When it was built, in 1760, Tynemouth House stood alone in its grounds. In 1839 plans were made to turn it into the Crown Hotel and pleasure gardens. The scheme fell through, and the land was laid out for building.

109. A dinner and the presentation of small souvenirs were the objects of a subscription fund set up for the men of Tynemouth Village who served in the South African Campaign of 1899 to 1902. So many contributions arrived, however, that it was decided to erect a memorial on the village green, at a cost of about £130. The chairman of the fund was J.M. Winter, and the designer was A.B. Plummer. On 13th October 1903, William S.F. Brodrick, lately Minister for War, visited Tynemouth to unveil the monument. He pointed out that the memorial was unusual, in that it included the names of all who had volunteered to fight in the Boer War.

110. The existence of the castle must have made the people of Tynemouth well-acquainted with the activities of the military; so well-acquainted, perhaps, that it was thought unnecessary to note the nature of the event recorded here. On the far side of the village green is Huntington Place, and the building with the large stone portico is Tynemouth House. The terrace was built in the grounds in the 1840s. In the mid-1860s it became Thomas White's boarding school. He was succeeded by the Reverend T.B. Nicholls in 1886, when Saint Oswald's College was transferred from Cullercoats. The name was changed to Tynemouth School in the 1890s, and more recently to King's School.

111. Two of the early electric trams belonging to the Tynemouth and District Electric Traction Company pass each other in Front Street. The photograph is dated between 1902, when Queen Victoria's memorial was erected, and about 1909, when Mason and Son ceased to keep the shop on the corner. Frederick Mason was born in Norwich, but worked at a flour mill in North Shields in the 1860s. In about 1870 he set up his own bakery there, and later opened branches in Tynemouth, Cullercoats and Whitley Bay. When he died in 1905 he had eight large shops and a large bakery.

Victoria Monument,   Tynemouth.

112. Queen Victoria's memorial in Tynemouth was recorded even before the full inscription was carved on the plinth, and long before the crown disappeared. Following her death in 1901, memorial statues proliferated. The second in the North of England was at Tynemouth. Almost £1,000 was subscribed by the people of the Borough of Tynemouth, in order to purchase from Alfred Turner, of Kensington, a copy of the statue erected in Delhi. A problem arose; the residents of Northumberland Square, North Shields, objected to it being placed in their gardens. The memorial was eventually unveiled on the village green on 25th October 1902.

113. Beyond the group of children is 7 Front Street. Until the 1860s it was the Star and Garter Inn, but by 1871 it had been re-named 'St. Oswin's', and was the home of William Henry Scott. He was the head of the Newcastle firm of merchants and shipowners, Scott Brothers. At the time of his death in 1902 he was known on the Quayside as the "Father of the 'Change". A later occupant was Ronald Cochran Stevenson, nephew of one of his partners. Mister Stevenson was a director of a local newspaper group. During 1905 he was active in setting up the Tyne Division of the Royal Naval Volunteer Reserve.

Front Street, Tynemouth.

Published by B. Graham, Whitley Bay.

114. The sign above the building to the extreme right announces it to be a branch of the North Shields Co-operative Society Limited. The Society was formed in 1860, and had members as far away as Whitley Bay. As it was reported that the Tynemouth members felt slighted by the opening of a branch in Cullercoats, some houses were bought on Front Street, and demolished. The new branch opened on 15th June 1904. The venture was not as successful as had been hoped, and for many years it lay idle. It was sold to the Tynemouth Social Club in 1920.

115. At one time the north side of Front Street was unbroken at this point. In the centre were a number of small houses around Percy Court, and beyond were fields down to the sea. In the early 1870s, the houses were demolished to allow the building of Percy Park Road. The café was, for many years, the property of Frederick Mason and Son, bakers. Opposite was Victor Walton and Company Limited, who later moved into Mason's premises. The corner properties are best remembered for the firms in occupation here. About 1920 Carrick's Dairy Company opened the café, and at the same time Maynard's, the confectionery chain, took the shop on the other side.

116. The view down Percy Park Road, towards Front Street, in about 1905, is recognizable, but the old businesses have disappeared. To the left, something of the sort was happening at the time. William Wallace Bell has only replaced one of the signboards of Thomas Oliver Mawson, chemist and druggist. Earlier the shop had been the premises of Mawson, Swan and Weddell, manufacturers of Cerebos Salt. In the centre, the Swiss House was established as a wine and spirit merchant's in 1898, by Martha Mather. The turreted building was for many years the Priory and Army Institute, connected with Holy Saviour's Church.

Front Street, Tynemouth

117. The driver of the horse-cart risked incurring a fine for leaving his animal unattended in the street outside Thomas Willits' fruit and fish shop. Perhaps he should have taken advantage of the stabling offered behind the Salutation Inn, through the alleyway to the left. In this most commercial section of Front Street, however, no-one is showing much concern. The section of street to the left included the bank, the old Bath Hotel, the Post Office, a large draper's shop, and a chain grocery. The striped blinds hide two old village businesses, Champney, the butcher, and Vickers' fancy bazaar.

NAVAL FUNERAL, TYNEMOUTH.

118. The Channel Fleet paid a short visit to the Tyne in 1904, their departure being delayed by the death aboard H.M.S. 'Hannibal' of Able Seaman John Arthur. His coffin was landed at the North Pier on 29th September, and the cortege passed along Front Street, on its way to Preston Cemetery. One of a series of postcards of the event, the picture shows the procession passing the Cumberland Arms, and Mrs Surtees' apartment house, which became Martin's Bank in the 1930s. In the centre is one of Walter Willson's grocery shops, and the building with the large signboard is Auty Limitied's shop and studio.

119. Auty Limited, photographers, claimed to be the first in the north of England to produce picture postcards. Matthew Auty started in business as a tobacco dealer at Tynemouth Place. In his spare time he took up photography as a hobby. About 1883 he abandoned the tobacco business and set up his studio at 20 Front Street. His reputation as a portraitist was such that people would travel many miles to sit for him. His landscape work sold throughout the North-East. Never a well man, he made provision for his business to become a limited company at his death, which took place on 29th July 1895.

PS396-7   RAPID C°

TYNEMOUTH FRONT ST. LOOKING EAST

120. According to the postmark, the photograph must have been taken during the first half of July 1910, or earlier. To the left is part of Auty's photography studio. The white door next to it is presumably to a café above Adam Nicholson's confectionery shop. It became Greenwell's drapery before the First World War. Beyond it would be the long established fruitshop of Thomas Crocker, and next door to that are the white tiles in front of Robert Champney's equally long lasting butcher's shop. To the right, it is just possible to see the sign of William James Bell, chemist in Front Street from about 1902 to the 1920s.

121. The Percy Arms Inn has stood at 25 Front Street, on the corner with Cross Street, since at least the 1820s, long before the 1930s frontage was put up. In the 1850s the landlord was John Hutchinson, previously of the Sea Water Baths in Prior's Haven. His son, John, is believed to have taken over the public house during the 1860s. John Hutchinson, the younger, in addition to being an innkeeper, was also a cab proprietor, a substantial builder and contractor, and a Councillor from 1887 to 1893. He died in 1897 and his son, William, took over briefly.

122. One building on Front Street has hardly changed since about 1905. At that time the white-fronted shop was Captain William Benjamin Brown's fish and poultry shop, which he ran from the 1890s to the 1930s. It was then taken over by Walter Marshall, under which name it is still familiar. Next door, to the left, was Miss Spence's studio, where she probably carved the North Shields Wooden Dolly for the 1902 Coronation. The building with the Hovis sign was Armstrong's Temperance Hotel from the 1850s to the 1880s, and thereafter it was divided. The tallest building on this part of the street was the Wesleyan Methodist Chapel, opened in 1870.

123. Robert Bell Armstrong opened a temperance hotel at what was then 69 Front Street in about 1850. After his death in 1875 it was run by his widow, Margaret Armstrong. In the 1880s the old hotel was divided, but part of the building retained a connection with the catering industry, by becoming a bakery. When the photograph was taken, in the early 1920s, the shop was being run by John J. Hewitt. In the Second World War the shop was requisitioned for use as a British Restaurant. After a short period as a school, it became Tynemouth Branch Library in 1953.

124. The classic Renaissance-style Wesleyan Methodist Chapel was opened in Front Street in 1870, replacing an older building in Percy Street, which later became the Priory Theatre. In 1935 the Front Street chapel became the Carlton Cinema, which was replaced in recent years by Timothy Duff Court. To the right of the chapel is James Fry's Fancy Emporium. The Frys were a family of boatmen, descended from William Fry, of Kent, who did much to develop the village as a tourist resort. One of them, James Fry, was a diver on the building of the North Pier, and did much to establish the family in the salvage diving business.

125. The large signboard over the Turk's Head Inn dates the photograph during the period when it was run by Andrew Nichol Dodd's firm, until about 1910. The public house is, perhaps, best known as the last resting place of Wandering Willie. He was a sheepdog accidentally left behind by a drover crossing the Tyne on the North Shields ferry. Between 1873 and 1880 Willie travelled the ferries, looking for his shepherd, and on two occasions just missed him. Suspicious of all at first, he came to allow the passengers and ferrymen to care for him. After his death the body was stuffed, and placed in the Turk's Head.

126. William Scott, of London, came to regard Tynemouth as his favourite resort, and in seeking to mark his appreciation, hit upon the idea of providing a drinking fountain in the heart of the village. A competition was held for the design, and it was won by the Newcastle architects, Oliver and Lamb. They engaged the services of Robert Beall, sculptor, and B.C. Lawton, builder. A public opening ceremony was held on 2nd September 1861. In those days the fountain had a thermometer and a barometer, in addition to the clock. In later years the fountain was used to hang a red lamp when the Life Brigade was on watch.

FRONT STREET. TYNEMOUTH. 217.

127. A turn of the century view from Tynemouth Castle includes two streets recorded as far back as Tudor times. Only one other existed in the village at that time. After the Second World War, much of the eastern end of Percy Street, to the right, was replaced by the car park opposite the Gibraltar Rock Inn. Also demolished was the block of substantial buildings between Percy Street and Front Street. When the picture was taken, one of them was William Mann Bell's cocoa rooms, and the other a confectioner's, selling Vose's Tynemouth Rock. To the left, a block of four houses, with dormers, stood on the site of the lawn outside the Roman Catholic church.

128. The triumphal arch at the top of Pier Road was probably erected for the visit of Albert Edward, Prince of Wales, on the occasion of the opening of the Albert Edward Dock at North Shields. On 21st August 1884 the Royal party set off on the ship 'Para 'e Amazonas', from Newcastle Quayside, and, having declared the dock open, proceeded down river to the North Pier. The procession moved under the arch, along East Street, through Percy Gardens, and thence to the railway station, via Percy Park, Manor Road and Front Street.

129. Following the Dissolution of the Priory in 1539, no Roman Catholic Mass was said in a consecrated building in the village for over three hundred years. Services were held at North Shields from 1784, and Saint Cuthbert's Church opened there in 1821. Canon Bewick, of Tynemouth, later Bishop of Hexham and Newcastle, wished to found a new church and monastery at Tynemouth, but funds were not forthcoming. A temporary church was opened behind 49 Front Street in 1871, but it was too small to deal with the influx of summer visitors. On 7th September 1889, the foundation stone of the present church was laid.

Front Street, East.

Tynemouth.

130. The Salutation is said to have been a coaching inn, and seems hardly to have changed its outward
appearance from those days. Next door is 61 Front Street, for many years the home of Charles
George. Born in the village in 1872, he studied art in Brussels, but had to give it up as a full-time occupation to take over his father's decorating business, in 1890. He was a prolific landscape artist, until
his death in 1937. The Local Studies Centre at North Shields has a window from the house with a poem
scratched into the glass, reputedly by Lady Byron. She stayed at the house whilst visiting the writer on
social issues, Harriet Martineau, who lived at 57 Front Street from 1839 to 1844.

131. Standing out to the left is a sign for the Bath Hotel, and just beyond it is the draper's shop which was the original Bath Inn. It was associated with the Sea Water Baths built in Prior's Haven in 1807, and thus was one of the oldest ventures in the tourist industry in the village. The arcade to the left leads through to Bath Terrace and to Bath Assembly Rooms, opened in the 1860s. To the left of the arcade, the building which in more recent years has been a restaurant, was a long established chemist's shop. The picture includes the name of Arthur Dagg, who followed William James Bell in occupation, in the early 1920s. The Post Office was on that site for only a few years in the mid-1920s.

132. A mark of the transition from rural village to dormitory town was the appearance in Front Street of larger, more fashionable shops. One of the earliest was opened at 71 Front Street by James Young, in 1881. His London Drapery House aimed to make all the latest fashions and materials available to the residents of the coastal towns. To that end he opened a branch at the even smaller village of Whitley, itself just beginning to grow. The firm was styled Young and Company after 1895, and seems to have been photographed before 1902, as Queen Victoria's Memorial is not evident in the background.

133. To those familiar with the village, the Congregational Church looks curiously truncated without its spire, as it was when it opened. By the 1860s, the growing body of Nonconformists in the area had only the old Wesleyan chapel in Percy Street to serve their needs, and that was unable to cope with the summer visitors. Francis C. Marshall, an engineer living nearby, was able to secure the corner site for the Congregationalists in October 1865. The foundation stones of the new church were laid in 1866. It was to be constructed in the Gothic style, to designs by Thomas Oliver, a Newcastle architect.

134. The Congregational Church was publicly opened on 3rd June 1868, but it was not to gain its spire until the winter of 1873. The need for a church hall was keenly felt, as the churches played an important part in the social life of the village. In about 1884 the two houses next to the church were bought for this purpose, but later demolished and replaced by Saint Oswin's Hall. In latter years only the hall was in regular use, and the church was converted into a shopping arcade. Next to Saint Oswin's Hall is the birthplace of a Tyneside chain of grocery shops. Allards Stores began there in 1880 as Wilson and Allard.

135. Almost invisible to the unaided eye, the photographer has recorded the shop signs of Howitt's ironmongery, and Mason's Café at the corner of Percy Park Road, in the distance. This dates the picture between 1901 and 1909. It was, perhaps, taken when Charles John Denham Christie was resident at 'Woodside', Colbeck Terrace; the house to the right. Mister Christie came to Tyneside in 1860, as manager of the new shipbuilding firm of Wigham Richardson. When it amalgamated with Swan and Hunter, to become one of the most famous shipyards in the world, he was one of the directors. He died here in 1905.

136. Tynemouth Railway Station stands at the western side of the village, approached from Front Street or Colbeck Terrace. Despite the complaints of local shopkeepers over the years, that the railways were carrying away their trade to Newcastle, the easy access they provided was vital in the growth of Tynemouth. Excursion traffic developed the resort, and commuter trains encouraged people to make their homes at the coast. The large station, now only partly used by the Tyneside Metro, was opened to deal with the greater volume of traffic in 1882.

137. *The day was prolific in incident, sublimity, fun, gaiety, and madness,... more character was developed, more wine was drank, more jollity felt, more rain descended, more thunder rolled, and lightning flashed, more men made fools of themselves, and more ladies got soaked to the skin than has perhaps occurred in the memory of the present generation.* Thus a reporter summed up the opening of the Newcastle and North Shields Railway in 1839, and the luncheon in a tent at Tynemouth House which followed. The line was extended to this, the Oxford Street terminus, in 1847. Given Sarah Owen's advertisement of the Royal Hotel, the picture may date from the early 1880s.

138. Tynemouth once had two railway stations. The first opened at Oxford Street in 1847, and second was a terminus for the Blyth and Tyne Railway Company, near the Master Mariners' Asylum, opened in 1860. This was replaced by a new station opposite Oxford Street, in 1864. Ten years later both lines were taken over by the North Eastern Railway Company, who set about building the present loop line from Newcastle to the coast. The magnificent glass and iron canopy was the showpiece of their station opened at Tynemouth in 1882. As a major tourist centre, special efforts were made at Tynemouth, and the staff regularly won prizes for their floral decorations.

139. Many thousands of passengers over the years would remember Tynemouth Station as the starting place of their holidays, but it also had a more workaday function. The nearby town of North Shields was one of the country's leading fishing ports. The position of the Fish Quay at the bottom of the steep river banks made easy access for railways impossible, and consequently fish had to be brought by cart to Tynemouth for distribution around the country. Before lorries became common the railway companies even maintained chain horses, to assist the dealers' carts up Tanner's Bank.

140. Much emphasis was laid on the efficiency of electricity when the Metro service was opened in 1980, but the loop line had been electrified once before. Due to competition from the various tramways in the area, the North Eastern Railway Company opened an electric train service in 1904. Faster and more comfortable journies were promised. Possibly it was to this end that they banned the fishwives of Cullercoats from carrying their wares aboard during the rush hour, thereby provoking a series of indignant letters to the press. The electric trains continued in service until 1963, when they were replaced by diesel units. From 1980 the Metro provided a fast service, co-ordinated with local buses.